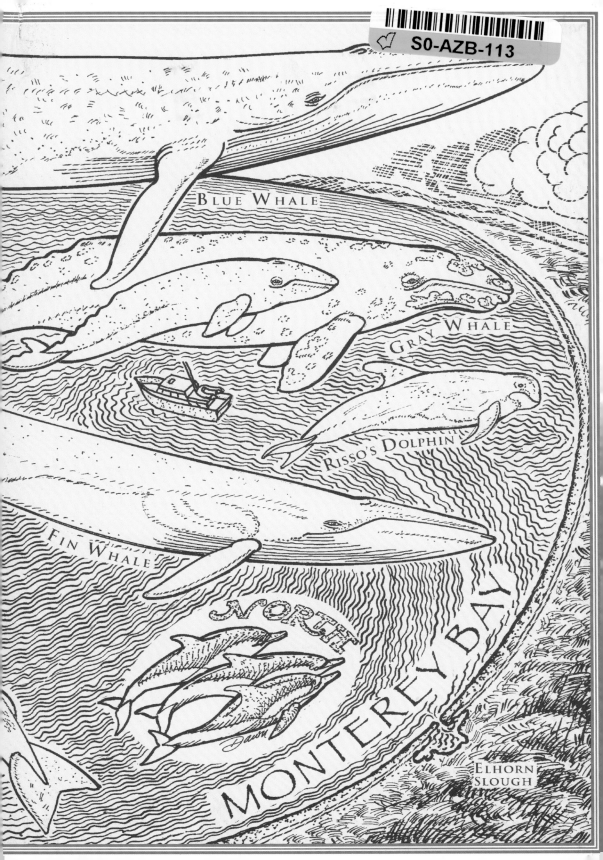

BLUE WHALE

GRAY WHALE

RISSO'S DOLPHIN

FIN WHALE

NORTH

MONTEREY BAY

ELHORN SLOUGH

Dawn

First Edition 2010
Produced and published by

BLUE OCEAN INSTITUTE

BLUE OCEAN INSTITUTE & MANTA PUBLICATIONS

Book Editor, Dominique Navarro
Juvenile Book Editor, Gay Ver Steeg
Book Production Associate, Megan Smith

Library of Congress Control Number: 2009908723
Nina Delmar -The Great WHALE Rescue

ISBN-978-0-9785417-0-5

"Our children must learn to save
the oceans with us." Dr. Sylvia Earle.

Thanks to Alexandra,
Dominique and Elizabeth
who are the next wave.

Nina Delmar

THE GREAT
WHALE
rescue

written by
Carl Safina

illustrated by
Dawn E. Navarro

Chapter One

The Longest Hour

There was no time to waste. And yet it would be at least another *hour* before they could reach the drowning whale. If only they could go *faster!*

But they couldn't. The wind was getting stronger, the seas growing higher. Waves pounded and shook the boat as it struggled forward toward the site of the distress call.

Nina Delmar wasn't even sure she could hang on. She wasn't the only one. Captain Carlo gripped the wheel intently.

"If this storm keeps up like this," he yelled over the sound of crashing waves to Nina, "I'm not sure we can keep going. We might have to turn back."

Nina looked up at him with disbelief. "But—we can't turn around!" protested Nina. "That would be giving up!"

"For our own safety," is all Captain Carlo could say. He knew Nina understood what was happening. Even poor Sombra—trembling with fear—knew they were in danger.

Nina felt many different things at once. She wanted to keep going. But she was also afraid. She was thankful the captain would keep their safety first. But if they had to turn around—if they could not get out to where the whale needed help—how sad would that be?

Even though it wouldn't be their fault, she felt she'd never forgive herself if the tangled-up whale drowned because they couldn't reach it.

"Why couldn't this have happened yesterday?" she thought just as another wave hit violently, causing Nina nearly to lose her balance, forcing her to hold tighter than ever, and sending so much green seawater across the windshield that for a few seconds no one could see anything.

Yesterday, the weather had been perfect. Everything was calm and blue; blue ocean, blue sky, with white clouds like fluffy cotton candy right from Fishermen's Wharf. Monterey Bay had never looked so beautiful, she'd thought.

Nina's grandfather and Captain Carlo's father had made their livings fishing together. So Nina had grown up near the sea. Sort of grown up, that is; she was almost eleven, not fully grown up, not *yet*. But in one way Nina was grown up: she knew what she liked.

She liked animals, mainly.

She liked trees, also mainly.

But she liked the sea mostly.

In fact she LOVED all these things so much, she had a hard time deciding her favorite. Yesterday the Pacific Ocean looked just so *beautiful* she'd finally decided: she loved the sea most of all. You could visit your favorite tree, and count on it being pretty much the same. She liked that. Your favorite dog: always loyal and dependably the same, and that is good, too.

But the sea was never the same. Not ever. You never knew, from one day to the next, how it would be—some days calm, sometimes rough, sometimes stormy. It could be simply fun one day, dangerous the next. It could be blue or gray or green, sometimes peaceful, sometimes scary. *The sea isn't just a different world,"* she thought; *"it's many different worlds."* And the life—so many kinds, from sea lions to seaweeds. In the tide pools she could find crabs and flowery anemonies. Or she could take her kayak along the kelp and the rocks, seeing oystercatchers and otters and—

"*Monterey Queen,
Monterey Queen,"*
blared the two-way radio.
"This is *Mighty Sardine.*
Do you copy?"

A huge wave struck the boat, making whitewater explode in all directions. The radio went unanswered as Nina and Captain Carlo just hung on.

Then the captain reached for the mike, pressed the key, and answered, *"Mighty Sardine,* this is *Monterey Queen.* Over."

"I am still wit' de whale," answered the accented voice on the radio. "She not looking good. She very tangled in ropes and stuff. Even her mouth, all tangled. We have no diving gear. We cannot help her. Ovah."

"We're doing our best, Ernesto," Captain Carlo told the fisherman. "But we're going right into the teeth of this wind. These seas are fighting us. I'm not even sure we can keep going. If it gets any worse—safety of the crew, y'know. Over."

"I understand." The radio crackled and faded, then came back. "We wait for you. Seas are bad here too. But I'll try to stay wit' her, long as I can." Ernesto looked out his boat's window at the whale, then pressed the microphone key again. "She getting exhausted. And wit' de seas kicked up like dis, she having trouble staying near de surface, having trouble breathing. She gonna need help soon or—.

Nina's eyes filled with tears- it was only a matter of time before: Too Late!

"What's your position,?" Ernesto asked. "Ovah."

Nina looked at the GPS. "Tell him we have ten miles to go," she said to Captain Carlo. She looked at the GPS again and could hardly believe her eyes. Four knots! *"Are we really going that slow?"* she wondered. On a good day—on a day like yesterday—they'd be there in under an hour. But this wasn't a good day so far.

It was true. The Captain radioed, *"Mighty Sardine*, this is the *Queen*. We're lookin' at ten miles, but it's gonna take us another two, two and a half hours—if we don't have to turn back."

Common Tern
Sterna hirundo

"Well," fisherman Ernesto radioed back, "Unless you tell me you have to turn around, I'll stay as long as de waves will let me. I am not going anywhere as long as you are still headed dis way. I feel bad for de whale."

Nina's heart sank; what if *Monterey Queen* couldn't get there? What if the whale drowned because they didn't get there *in time?* Whales can swim like fish, but because they're mammals they can't breathe underwater. They need to breathe at the surface, like us.

Captain Carlo looked at Nina with concern. "Nina," he said kindly, "you know I'm doing the best I can."

Looking straight through the window at the bleak, wind-whipped sea, Nina nodded, and wiped away her tears.

Chapter Two

Whale Sighting

Fisherman Ernesto had been headed for home aboard the *Mighty Sardine* when he saw a whale that seemed to be in trouble. Ernesto had caught a load of Dungeness crabs and was in a hurry to get them to market. But he slowed down and picked up his binoculars and stepped out of the wheelhouse for a better look. The whale rolled on its side and he saw its long flippers, so he knew it was a Humpback Whale.

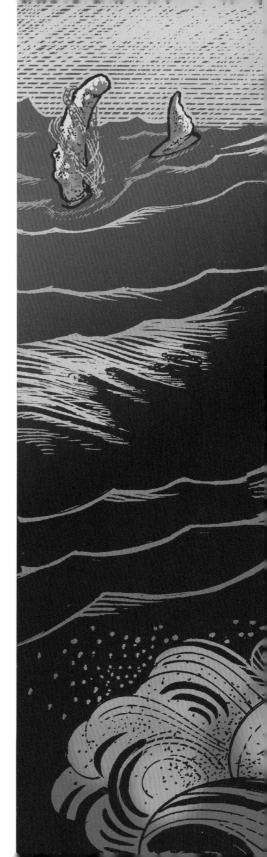

Only when the whale tried lifting its tail did Ernesto see exactly what the problem was. The whale was all tangled up—in crab trap lines! Ernesto knew the whale wasn't tangled up in his own lines, but the sight made him feel awful. Ernesto didn't like it when his fishing gear caught or hurt or tangled things he wasn't trying to catch. But he knew it happened. And now this. Fisherman Ernesto always enjoyed seeing whales. He just hated to see this great, innocent creature struggling. He knew the whale could not survive dragging heavy crab traps and ropes like that.

Ernesto immediately called Captain Carlo. Would he consider getting some divers and coming out in this storm to try to rescue this whale?

12

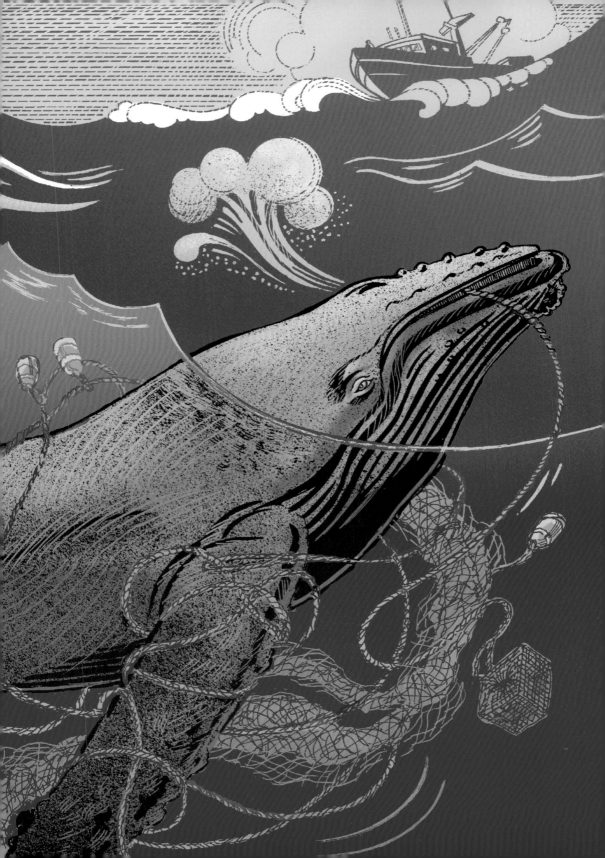

No one loved whales more than Nina.

She loved them so much, she had read every book on them she could find . Sometimes, she didn't like what she read. She'd read that in the past, especially in the 1800s and 1900s, there were fishermen called "whalers" who'd hunted whales around the world until there were almost none left. It wasn't until 1986 that most countries finally agreed to stop such hunting. But even today, countries like Japan are still killing whales. To Nina, that made *no* sense. She was very thankful that she lived in a part of the world where whales are protected, where most are recovering from the hunting of past times.

Nina could still remember her first whale sighting. She was standing on the cliffs at Point Lobos, staring out at the ocean with its kelp beds

Common Murre
Uria aalge

waving in the swells below her, the sound of the crashing waves in her ears, and the wind blowing back her braids. Suddenly, a great spout of steamy air shot from the sea as a Gray Whale surfaced. Beside it, a "little" Gray Whale baby, with a little spout of breath. These gray whales were migrating from the lagoons of Mexico, where the babies are born, all the way to Alaska for the summertime! Nina wished she could travel along with the whales. And even though whale babies are already bigger than almost any kind of grown-up animal, Nina thought it was the cutest baby she'd ever seen.

And Nina had seen Humpback whales hurling their 50-foot bodies into the air, crashing down and throwing spray like school buses falling from the sky She'd seen sleek Minke whales, whose name rhymes with slinky. She'd seen Finback Whales, sometimes *seventy feet* long. And, once, Nina saw two massive, blunt-headed Sperm Whales who'd come into Monterey Bay hunting the big Humboldt Squid. The squid live where it is so deep the water is always cold and very dark—even in daytime. Nina read that Humboldt Squid grow up to *twelve feet* long, the length of two tall men standing on top of each other. That seemed impossible! But, she thought, *whales* seem impossible too.

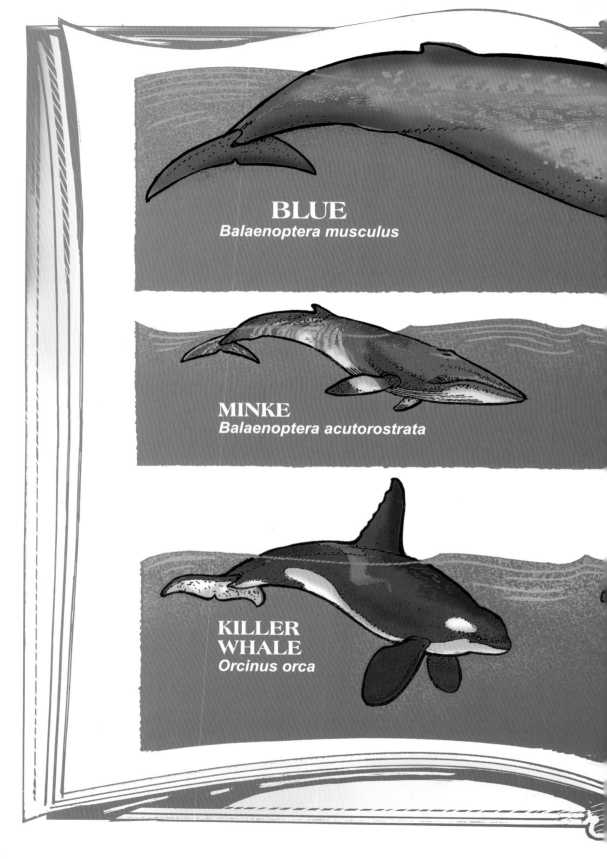

BLUE
Balaenoptera musculus

MINKE
Balaenoptera acutorostrata

**KILLER
WHALE**
Orcinus orca

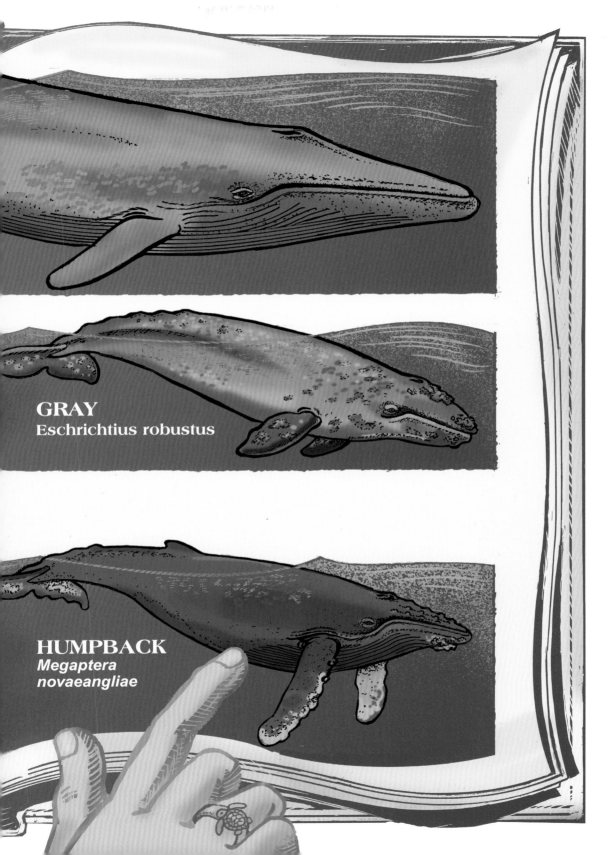

GRAY
Eschrichtius robustus

HUMPBACK
Megaptera novaeangliae

In fact, Nina thought one of the greatest things about the sea was that so many things that seem nearly impossible live here. Nina had seen—on calm days—Ocean Sunfish up to ten feet long, weighing up to *two tons*, as much as two small cars. To Nina they looked like huge fish sawed in half. They certainly seemed impossible. And how about Leatherback turtles that can weigh 2,000 pounds? Nina'd seen a couple of them. They looked like dark green Volkswagen Beetles with heads the size of basketballs. First time she saw one, Nina could hardly believe a turtle could get that big!

HAWKSBILL SEA TURTLE

GREEN SEA TURTLE

LEATHERBACK
SEA TURTLE

But the one thing Nina couldn't *ever* get over was that right here lived the biggest, most huge animal that has *ever* lived on Earth—bigger than any dinosaur. *"Ladies and gentlemen,"* Nina thought whenever she saw one (because it always seemed that the biggest animal that ever lived should always be announced to the whole world), *"please welcome—The Blue Whale!"* When they blew, their breath was an enormous cone of steam. Blues made other whales look *small*, which to Nina seemed just crazy.

"I don't know about this, Nina." Captain Carlo's voice brought Nina's thoughts flashing back to the crisis. "I want to do this as much as you do, but—." He switched the radio dial to check the ocean weather forecast. The voice came crackling into the pilothouse. They both heard, "…winds out of the northwest averaging 25 knots this morning, with seas six to eight feet. Winds decreasing to 10 to 15 knots by afternoon, seas diminishing to four feet…"

"Did you hear that Sombra?," Nina said. "The weather's going to get better."

Chapter Three

Excited
and
Scared

A few minutes
later, the sound of the wind,
which had been whistling
in the boat's antennas for
hours, started quieting.
The waves began relaxing.
Captain Carlo smiled at
Nina, pushed the throttle
forward, and as the
boat picked up speed
he yelled,
"Nina Delmar,
to the rescue!"

SEA BIRDS OF THE BAY

Captain Carlo took up the radio mike and called, "*Mighty Sardine,* this is the *Queen.* We're going faster, and getting closer. I think I see you up ahead now. Here we come."

Nina got on her tip-toes, and though the spray was flying, she thought she saw a speck on the horizon that might be the *Mighty Sardine.*

"*Queen,*" radioed Ernesto. "The whale, she lookin' very exhausted. Please get your crew here as fast as you can."

Nina had never been more excited and scared at the same time. No one knew what would happen when they got to the ailing whale, or how things might turn out. Nina only knew this: she was about to do the most dangerous thing of her life.

"We're crossing the canyon now," Captain Carlo said. "We should start seeing some life."

"Look for *life,*" Nina told Sombra. Monterey Canyon is like the Grand Canyon, but under deep water in the seafloor. The edge of the Canyon always seemed to have a lot of animals at home above and below the waves.

Nina started seeing flying cormorants with their long necks, and Pigeon Guillemot with their football-shaped bodies, white wing-patches and bright red legs. She saw Sooty Shearwaters who would flap and glide, flap and glide,

Sooty Shearwater
Puffinus grisens

○ SHEARWATER MIGRATION
○ MONTEREY BAY, CALIFORNIA

just above the rolling waves. These dark-feathered little shearwaters, Nina knew, come here all the way from New Zealand. That's where they've all hatched. Each year they cross the whole ocean to South America, then cross the ocean again from South America to the waters off Russia. From there they travel to Alaska and fly all the way down the coastline to these rich feeding areas of Monterey Bay before crossing the ocean one more time and returning to New Zealand. Nina thought that was just amazing—how far they travel, how hard they work to stay alive.

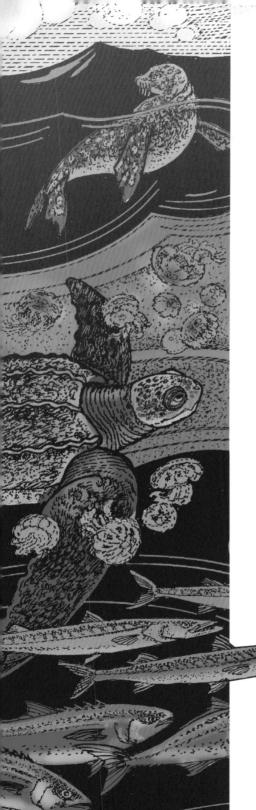

"Look," said Captain Carlo, gesturing with his chin as he kept both hands on the steering wheel. Suddenly a Black-footed Albatross with seven-foot-long wings crossed right in front of the boat, looking big in the windshield. Nina especially loved these birds, which seemed able to glide forever. She knew that they come all the way from islands past Hawaii, and that some of them come all this way— about 2,500 miles—just to find and bring food back to their chicks. Nina thought that was crazy. And that's what she loved; she loved this place because it was so crazy.

When they crossed the deepest part of the Canyon Nina saw so much commotion and splashing up ahead, at first she thought it was a huge flock of birds taking off from the water. But then she realized she was seeing not wings but fins, and that it was the

most dolphins she'd ever seen. There were hundreds. And they started leaping in the wake and playing in the bow wave. They seemed so full of life, they made Nina feel happy and hopeful for the first time all day.

A couple of sea lions popped up in the waves. Nina knew there are so many animals in Monterey Bay—the seabirds, dolphins, sea lions, and others—because the canyon's deep, steep slopes bring up nutrients that feed tiny plants and animals called plankton. Little shrimp-like creatures, called krill, eat the plankton. Many animals, including Blue Whales, eat the krill. Fish like salmon and sardines also eat krill. Then sea lions eat fish like sardines. And sea lions sometimes get eaten, too—by Great White Sharks. Nina knew that everything, from the smallest to the biggest, played a role. And, she suddenly realized, she had an important role to play too—to help save this whale.

But now Nina had Great White Sharks on her mind. Nina knew that to try to free the whale, people would have to get into the deep, chilly water. She had been hoping that Captain Carlo would let her join the team. She knew that if the weather stayed rough, or if the situation looked too dangerous, he wouldn't let her go into the water. She wanted badly to help, but she was also feeling scared. No one knew how the whale would react. Freeing the whale sounded good at first, but now that she thought about it, she was getting more nervous.

Black-footed Albatross
Diomedea nigripes

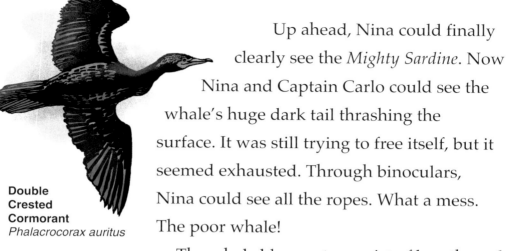

Double Crested Cormorant
Phalacrocorax auritus

Up ahead, Nina could finally clearly see the *Mighty Sardine*. Now Nina and Captain Carlo could see the whale's huge dark tail thrashing the surface. It was still trying to free itself, but it seemed exhausted. Through binoculars, Nina could see all the ropes. What a mess. The poor whale!

The whale blew a steamy jet of breath, and inhaled just before a wave rolled right over its head. It was dragging so much weight it could not get the top of its head safely above water. It was really struggling to stay at the surface. Nina could see that fisherman Ernesto was exactly right; this whale was running out of time.

Captain Carlo got on the intercom and called to the crew, "All hands on deck. We are approaching the whale. Bring your masks, fins, and snorkels, ready the Zodiac for launching, and be suited to dive."

Fisherman Ernesto's voice came over the radio. "It not gonna be easy to help this whale, Carlo," he said. "She wrapped in rope like a fly tangled in a spider web."

Captain Carlo could see she had hundreds of yards of rope wound around her whole body, especially around her tail. It looked bad. It looked like she was tangled in the lines of between 15 and 20 crab traps. That meant more than half a mile of heavy lines, not to mention the traps, which, at nearly 100 pounds each, added up to a ton of weight.

All the heavy crab traps were pulling the ropes tight. Nina could see that some of the ropes were so tight they were cutting through the whale's skin and into its flesh. The sight made her heartsick.

Her hopes sank. How in the world, she wondered, could they ever help this whale?

Underwater Mask and Snorkel

Nina needs two-3 pound weights on her weight belt for neutral buoyancy in the water.

To stay warm and protected in the cold water, Nina is wearing 5 layers: first her bathing suit layered under a full body lycra suit, then a 5 mm neoprene wet suit, then her 3 mm neoprene dive vest and her lucky sea turtle dive shorts.
AND
dive gloves, dive booties and fins.

To Captain Carlo, it looked like the whale needed all the help it could get, and fast. He turned to Nina and said, "Get your wetsuit on." Now Nina didn't have time to feel scared. She only knew she would give anything to save this whale, and now she had that chance.

She quickly zipped up her wet suit and joined the crew on the deck, ready to go. Nina was an excellent swimmer and snorkeler and tried to look confident. She noticed everyone on the rescue crew looked nervous too. Nobody had ever dealt with a situation like this before. No one had ever seen a whale in such trouble.

And no one knew how the whale would react to the divers—especially if it felt frightened. The female whale, about 50 feet long, weighing about one ton per foot, made Nina feel very small.

Fisherman Ernesto radioed again. "I've got some special heavy-duty rope clippers. They're awful good at cutting crab ropes. Head over in your Zodiac and I'll pass them down to you."

The crew got into the Zodiac and a crane lifted them—Zodiac and all—from the deck and over the side. The water had calmed down a lot but there were still some big waves, and one wave hit the *Monterey Queen* just as the Zodiac was being lowered. The crane cable swung and everyone held on tight as the rubber boat slammed into the side of the *Monterey Queen* and bounced off. As the Zodiac settled into the sea surface they immediately disconnected the cable hook and zoomed safely away from the rocking side of the *Queen*.

Nina was soon skimming over the waves with the other divers, holding the bow-rope for balance as they approached the rusty sides of the *Mighty Sardine*. Fisherman Ernesto was waiting. He lowered a mesh bag with four pairs of his special rope clippers. Nina took the bag and untied it. "Go, girl," Ernesto said with a big grin, "Go save that poor whale!"

Without another moment to think, they turned the Zodiac and approached the whale, who was bobbing exhausted at the surface.

As they drew close in their small boat, the whale made a sudden mighty thrash with her tail in a desperate attempt to break free of the ropes. Nina could see that one whack from that tail—even by accident—could injure and maybe even kill a person. Another danger was the possibility of getting tangled in those lines if the whale suddenly moved or rolled. And the whale had also tangled an old fishing net. If a person got tangled in any of the stuff the whale was tangled in, they could drown. Nina's mind flashed with doubts and fears. The idea, after all, had been to save a whale, not to get killed! And she wasn't sure—nobody was sure—they could cut off all the lines and crab traps and actually save the whale. What if they cut off some of them and the whale swam away with a lot of ropes still weighing her down; she might die anyway.

"OK," said the Zodiac driver, "Let's put one person in the water and see what the whale does. Nina, you stay here for now."

One of the divers slipped into the sea, swimming along the surface to where the whale was struggling to breathe.

And then, a strange thing happened: the whale did not thrash or lunge in fear. In fact, she seemed to relax a little.

The diver called out, "It looks terrible. I don't know if we'll be able to save her, but everyone grab your clippers and get in; let's start cutting off as much rope as we can."

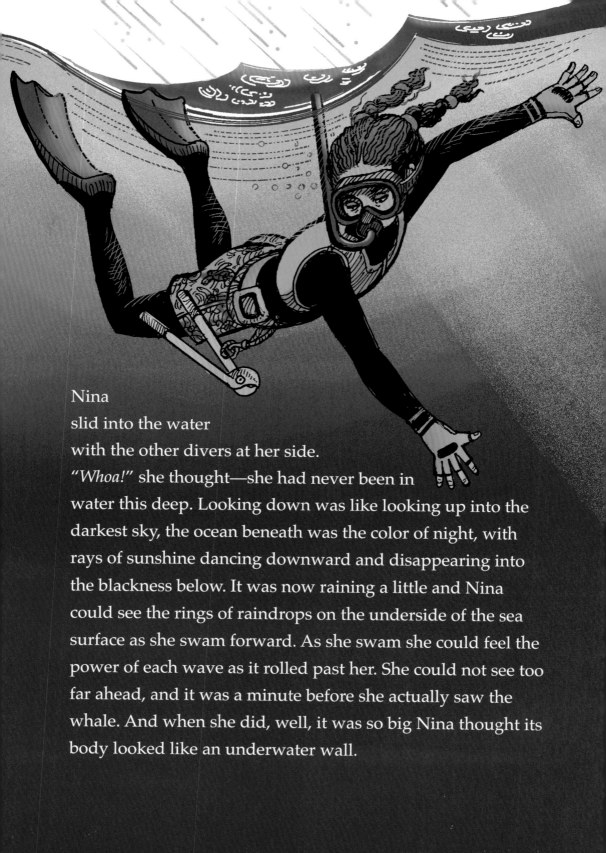

Nina
slid into the water
with the other divers at her side.
"Whoa!" she thought—she had never been in
water this deep. Looking down was like looking up into the
darkest sky, the ocean beneath was the color of night, with
rays of sunshine dancing downward and disappearing into
the blackness below. It was now raining a little and Nina
could see the rings of raindrops on the underside of the sea
surface as she swam forward. As she swam she could feel the
power of each wave as it rolled past her. She could not see too
far ahead, and it was a minute before she actually saw the
whale. And when she did, well, it was so big Nina thought its
body looked like an underwater wall.

Nina's heart was pounding as she swam right up to the whale and put her hand against its dark, wrinkled skin. It seemed soft and sensitive. She went to the surface and took a breath, then dove a few feet down, grabbed a rope, worked her clippers between the rope and the whale's skin, put both hands around the clipper's handles and squeezed with all her might. The rope was so tight it made a crease in the whale's skin. The clippers made a satisfying *SNAP!* as the rope popped apart. While Nina rose to take a breath, she watched as the rope she'd just cut and the crab trap that was attached to it sank out of sight.

All the divers were clipping lines around the whale's body and tail—which was still the most dangerous place to be working. They'd take a deep breath, go down a few feet, grab a rope where it was wound tight, cut it apart, rise to the surface for another deep breath, and cut some more. Most of the lines were wound around the whale so many times that they had to be cut again and again before they came fully free. But every time a crab trap sank or the tension on a rope slackened, the whale could breathe a little bit easier.

And now it seemed to all the divers, and to Captain Carlo and Fisherman Ernesto who were watching intently from their boats, that the whale understood that these people had come to help her. Many people have gone to sea to kill whales over the years. Sadly, some still do. But this whale understood that these people had come to save her life.

35

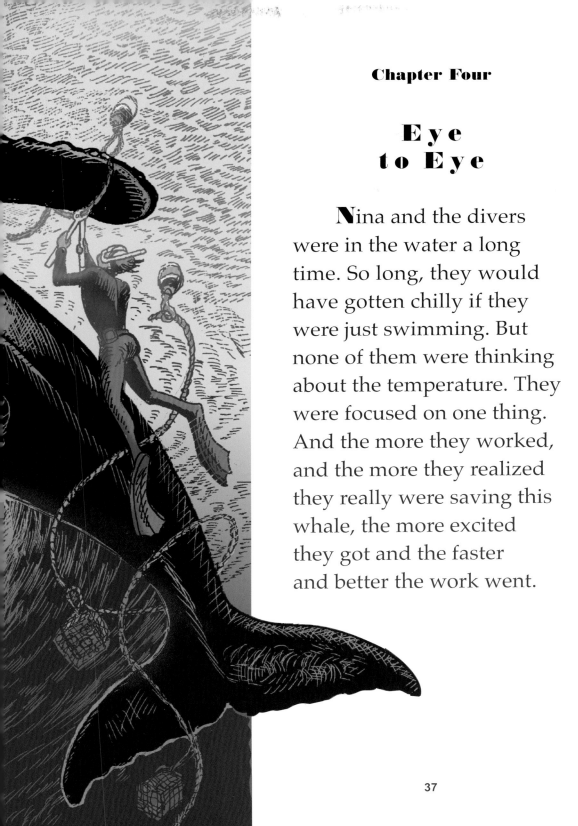

Chapter Four

Eye to Eye

Nina and the divers were in the water a long time. So long, they would have gotten chilly if they were just swimming. But none of them were thinking about the temperature. They were focused on one thing. And the more they worked, and the more they realized they really were saving this whale, the more excited they got and the faster and better the work went.

Nina had worked her way toward the whale's shoulder when she saw that there was a line tight across her tongue and jaw, with a big, heavy crab trap hanging from it.

The whale lifted her head a little, and Nina came eye to eye with her. Her eye, set in wrinkled skin, was huge and sad and frightened-looking. Nina almost forgot her task for a moment, staring into that big eye, wishing she could say something.

But actions speak louder than words, and the whale seemed to understand. Why else would she be staying still and quiet all this long time, waiting patiently and not trying to swim off, even after many of the lines had been cut?

Nina returned to the surface for a breath and then grabbed the rope that was digging into the corner of the whale's mouth. She pressed and pressed on the clippers but this rope was tougher. The whole time, just inches away, the whale's eye

was closely watching. But Nina could only fray the rope. She could not cut through it, and she needed more air. At the surface she breathed extra hard, and when she returned to work more strands of the rope started parting until—*clip!*, finally—the rope broke and the trap sank. Nina pulled the rest of the loose rope away from the whale's jaw.

The whale watched as Nina surfaced again. And as Nina blew out of her snorkel and inhaled again, the whale blew and inhaled too. Nina thought it strange and wonderful that she and the whale could look so different yet seem so similar, so alike.

The whale understood. Nina suddenly felt very sure this was true, more deeply true than any truth she had ever known before.

When Nina swam back toward the whale's tail to see how the other divers were doing, she realized she had cut the last rope; the whale was completely free!

They had done it!

Now the whale moved, but slowly, and deliberately. She was careful not to hit the divers with her tail, or hurt them in any way. And as she realized she was really, finally, fully free, she began swimming in circles. She dove under the divers. Nina and the others watched her whole huge body streaming by just beneath them.

Then the whale came up and nuzzled one of the divers. She swam in tight circles and came back to Nina and the others. Again and again she circled, came back, nudged them, and rubbed her

body gently along theirs. She reminded Nina of a happy, affectionate puppy—a 50-foot-long puppy.

Nina had loved whales a long time, but this whale was showing its love for Nina. Nina felt that in the whole world there could not possibly be anything that could feel better. The whale began swimming in bigger and bigger circles and eventually moved away, until her dark body disappeared into the darkness of the deep sea, and all Nina could see of her was her long whitish flippers that seemed to be waving goodbye. And soon, with a last wave, she was gone.

As she swam back to the Zodiac, Nina knew that this day that had started out so terribly had turned out perfect. *"Today was the best day ever,"* she thought. She knew it was a day she would never forget, as long as she lived.

When she climbed back aboard the Zodiac and was heading toward the *Monterey Queen* and Captain Carlo, she did not feel like just a little girl anymore. She had done something that mattered.

Everyone knew the whale would never be the same, that they'd changed its life. Nina knew one additional secret no one else did. She knew that the whale had changed her life, too. She knew she would never be the same, either.

On Wednesday, December 14, 2005 a story was published in the San Francisco Chronicle, written by staff writer Peter Fimrite. It read, "A humpback whale freed by divers from a tangle of crab trap lines near the Farallon Islands nudged its rescuers and flapped around them in what marine experts said was a rare and remarkable encounter."

READ MORE stories about whales and ocean animals:

Watch for real life stories printed in your local newspapers. Whale rescue attempts are happening worldwide as more and more people understand the plight of these gentle giants.

MORE information about Humpback Whales:
* Scientific Name: Megaptera novaeangliae
* Family: Baleen Whale
* Class: Marine Mammal
* Size: 48 to 60 ft (14.6 to 19 m)
* Weight: 40 tons (36 metric tons)

Scientists think there are only 80,000 humpback whales worldwide.

Humpback whales are known for their magical and complex songs, that may last for 10 to 20 minutes and then repeat for hours at a time. Scientists are studying these sounds to understand their meaning. Most likely humpbacks sing to communicate with others and to attract potential mates.

The humpback whale is often spotted along our coastlines, feeding on tiny shrimp-like krill, plankton and small fish. They migrate every year from summer feeding grounds near the North and South Poles, to warmer winter breeding waters close to the Equator. Mothers and their young swim close together, often affectionately touching one another with their flippers. Calves do not stop growing until they are ten years old.

Humpbacks are powerful, graceful swimmers. They use their massive tail fin, or fluke, to propel themselves through the water. Often they leap from the water, landing with a tremendous splash. Scientists aren't sure if this breaching behavior serves some purpose, or whether whales simply do it for fun. Whatever their reason, sighting a humpback whale and its huge splash is awesome.

Like all large whales, the humpback continues to be a target for the whaling industry. Due to over-hunting, its population fell by an estimated 90% before it got protection in 1966. Some whale species have since partially recovered. However, entanglement in fishing gear, collisions with ships, and noise and water pollution remain problems for all ocean animals.

Think about a career as a marine biologist or ocean scientist.

Saving whales and ocean mammals requires both science knowledge and a dedication to the animals. Check out the web and www.wikipedia.org to learn more about marine life professionals who have helped whales. Search for names such as International Whaling Commissioner Sidney Holt, Roger Payne who is famous for his work of recording whale songs and Diane Gendron who has dedicated her life to the study of the Eastern Pacific population of Blue Whales in the Gulf of California. And visit the site: **TOPP** at **www.topp.org** to see what is happening in the science of ocean predators!

MOST importantly have fun LEARNING about whales, dolphins, sea animals and their ocean habitats by visiting an aquarium, going on a whale-watch boat trip and by joining organizations that support whale and ocean education, conservation and research:

BLUE OCEAN INSTITUTE
www.blueocean.org

MONTEREY BAY AQUARIUM
www.montereybayaquarium.org

THE OCEAN ALLIANCE
www.oceanalliance.org

**SEA SHEPHERD
CONSERVATION
SOCIETY**
www.seashepherd.org

**Whale and Dolphin
Conservation Society
www.wdcs.org
www.whaleadoption.org/kids.asp**

Blue Whale *Balaenoptera musculus*
110 ft. Range: All oceans of the world.

Fin Whale *Balaenoptera physalis*
59-72 ft. Range: All oceans of the world.

Sei Whale *Balaenoptera borealis*
45-55 ft. Range: Antarctic, Iceland in the North Atlantic.

Bryde's Whale *Balaenoptera edeni*
45-55 ft. Range: Tropical and sub-tropical waters.

Minke Whale *Balaenoptera acutorostrata*
26-31 ft. Range: All oceans of the world.

Humpback Whale *Megaptera novaeangliae*
35-50 ft. Range: All oceans of the world.

Pygmy Sperm Whale *Kogia breviceps*
Range: All temperate, sub-tropical, tropical waters.

Sperm Whale *Physeter macrocephalus*
36-59 ft. Range: All oceans of the world.

Pygmy Right Whale
Caperea marginata
20 ft. Range: Temperate waters of the Southern hemisphere.

Right Whale *Eubalaena spp.*
36-59 ft. Range: All oceans of the world.

Bowhead Whale *Balaena mysticetus*
50 ft. Range: Always close to the edge of the Arctic icepack.

Baird's Beaked Whale *Berardius bairdii*
39-42 ft. Range: North Pacific.

Gray Whale *Eschrichtius robustus*
40-45 ft. Range: Eastern North Pacific.

Pilot Whale *Globicephala melaena*
12-20 ft. Range: Cold temperate and subpolar waters.

Cuvier's Beaked Whale *Ziphius cavirostris*
18 -23 ft. Range: All oceans of the world.

Narwhal *Monodon monoceros*
15 ft. Range: Northwest Atlantic region, Canada, Greenland.

Beluga Whale *Delphinapterus leucas*
14-16 ft. Range: Arctic and subarctic waters.

Orca - Killer Whale *Orcinus orca*
22-32 ft. Range: All oceans of the world.

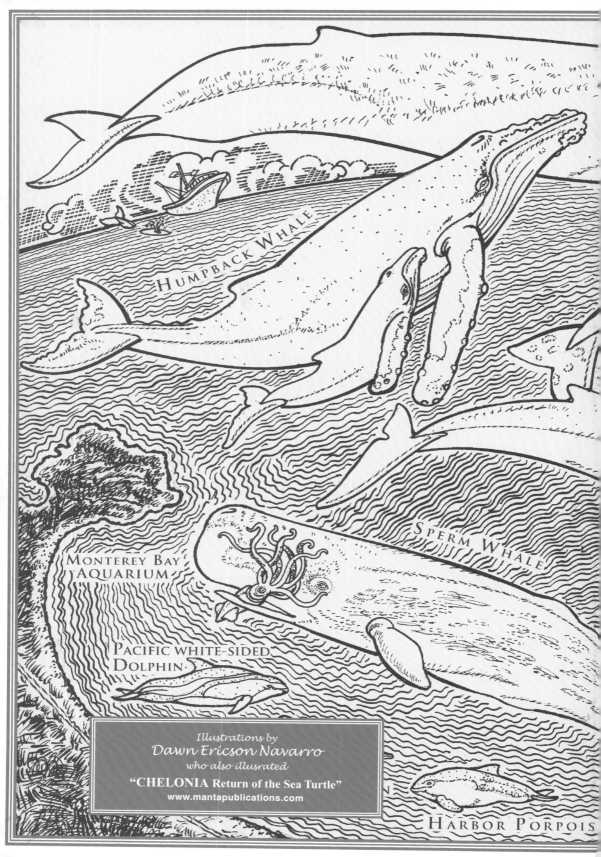

HUMPBACK WHALE

SPERM WHALE

MONTEREY BAY AQUARIUM

PACIFIC WHITE-SIDED DOLPHIN

HARBOR PORPOIS